For Tomorrow's Economists

Diya Mati

ILLUSTRATIONS BY - KOUSTUV MOHAPATRA

CONTENTS

ACKNOWLEDGEMENT

I am deeply grateful to all my teachers who have instilled in me a love for Economics. I also want to thank my sister, Isha Mati, a graduate in Economics from Cambridge University (UK), for her invaluable feedback and guidance. I am very appreciative of my cousin Koustuv Mohapatra for illustrating this book. Lastly, I am thankful for the support and guidance from my parents throughout this process.

PREFACE

Hi! I am Diya Mati, a student of grade 11 at Dhirubhai Ambani International School in Mumbai, India. My love for Economics began in grade 2 during a unit called "How We Organise Ourselves." Back then, my classmates and I worked on a project to help a small company survive against its competitor. It might sound like a big task for seven-year-olds, but we had a lot of fun making it happen!

In grade 10, I reignited this passion through my personal project, where I decided to write a children's book on Economics. I noticed that most schools in India don't have textbooks or curriculums to introduce young students to basic but essential economic concepts. Economics is a subject we encounter at every stage of our lives, from meeting our basic needs to using our resources sustainably. It's everywhere! Furthermore, economics is relevant on a global level, highlighting the interdependence of countries and how they trade, share resources, and solve problems together.

I believe introducing Economics at an early age can enhance real-world knowledge and understanding, and help young minds value financial aspects in their decision-making processes. I hope you enjoy reading this book and learn something new along the way!

CHAPTER 1:

THE BASICS OF ECONOMICS

Economics is a social science that studies how things are produced, transported, and consumed.

Production

Transportation

Consumption

It looks at how people, businesses, governments, and countries choose to use their limited resources. But let's start off by talking about what resources are.

In economics, the factors of production are the resources we use to produce **goods** or **services.**

Goods are physical items like pens and apples.

Services are activities done by people like a barber doing a haircut.

These are factors of production:

Land

The natural resources in an area including the land, sunlight, and air.

Labour

The physical and mental efforts taken while doing a job.

Capital

The machinery, tools, and equipment used. Money is also termed as capital.

Entrepreneurship

The ability of people to take ownership and make business decisions

For example, if I want to produce loaves of bread, I'll require...

Land

The agricultural land to grow wheat along with natural resources like sunlight and water

Labour

Workers required to plant, harvest, and process the wheat into flour, as well as to bake the bread

Capital

The agricultural tools
like tractors and mills,
as well as ovens
to bake bread and
overall money to buy
resources.

Entrepreneurship

A bread business owner
who makes decisions
for the company.

But there's a big challenge: Resources are limited, which means there's only so much land, labour, and capital available.

At the same time, people's needs and wants are unlimited—they always want more things.

Just like how these kids want more candies than what is available in the jar.

This creates the fundamental economic problem of scarcity. **Scarcity** means there are limited resources to fulfil our unlimited needs and wants.

Due to scarcity, we need to make choices.

When we choose to do or buy one thing, we have to give up the opportunity to do or buy something else. This is called the **opportunity cost.**

For example, if someone gives me ₹100 to spend on stationery, I need to choose the best way to spend this limited amount of money.

Pen   Pencil

Let's say I choose to buy 2 pens with my money. My opportunity cost would be 5 pencils because I could have bought 5 pencils with the same amount of money.

Let's take another example where I have ₹250 to spend on chocolates.

I'm currently debating between buying 5 small chocolates, or 1 medium and 2 small chocolates.

I finally decided to buy the second combination, and purchase 1 medium and 2 small chocolates.

Now, my opportunity cost will be what I would have gotten with my next best combination of chocolates, which is 5 small chocolates.

So, we can understand that opportunity cost is the value we would have gained by choosing the next best alternative.

CHAPTER 2:

SUPPLY AND DEMAND

Let's say I'm organising a bake sale.

I have 20 cupcakes ready to sell at ₹50 each. This is called my supply. As a producer, I control supply.

There are 30 people ready to buy my cupcakes at ₹50 each. This is called the **demand** and the people purchasing my products are called **consumers**.

In this case, my demand (30 cupcakes) is greater than my supply (20 cupcakes). This means that people want more of my product than what is available.

This is called a **shortage**.

When this occurs, as an entrepreneur, I can make some decisions. For example, I can increase the price. Let's say I'll increase my price to ₹60.

At this higher price point, less people would be willing to buy the cupcakes. Now, maybe only 15 people want to buy my cupcakes.

Now, my supply is 20 cupcakes but my demand is only 15 cupcakes. This means that the demand is less than the supply.

This situation is called a **surplus.**

I now need more consumers to be willing to purchase my cupcakes. So, I will decrease my price to ₹55.

Finally, I have 20 consumers willing to purchase my product. At this point, we say the market is at **equilibrium** because the supply and demand are equal.

Now imagine I, as a producer, want to increase the demand without changing my price. How might I do this?

I can tell everyone at school about my bake sale, showing them pictures of my delicious cupcakes. More people might come to buy them because they know about it. This is called **advertising.**

I could also say, "Buy one cupcake, get one free!" This makes people think they are getting a better deal, so they might buy more cupcakes. This is called an **offer.**

I could make special cupcakes with fancy decorations or unique flavours that no one else has. This makes my cupcakes different from others, so more people might want to try them. This is called **product differentiation.**

Producers use these techniques to increase the demand without changing prices.

CHAPTER 3

THE CIRCULAR FLOW MODEL

This is a household.

It comprises people that live in a house and can make financial decisions.

Households own the factors of production. For example...

Your family may own a plot of **land** that they can rent out or sell.

The adults in your family can work and have jobs, meaning they are the **labour** themselves.

Your parents have financial **capital,** or money that they can save and invest with.

Someone in your family could be a businessperson, or an **entrepreneur.**

This is a firm.

Households sell factors of production to firms so that the firms can produce goods and services.

In exchange for factors of production, firms give households:

Rent when they receive land

Wages to pay for labour

Interest for capital

Profit for entrepreneurs

Households also give money to firms by spending money on purchasing goods and services. This is called **consumer expenditure.**

In return, firms give households the goods and services to enjoy.

So, if we want to map out how money flows from households to firms and back, we can make a chart something like this:

When we look at the way that only households and firms interact, we are looking at a **closed economy.**

In the real world, money goes to other sectors too like...

The government

Banks

The foreign sector (other countries)

In this way, the economy works in a big circular motion where different sectors give and take money from each other.

Everyone depends on each other to keep the circular flow going. So, when you buy something, someone else gets money, and the cycle continues. This is how our economy works like a big, connected system!

CHAPTER 4:

TAXES

Taxes are like a fee we pay to the government.

They help the government build roads, schools, hospitals, and spend money on projects that the community needs.

There are different types of taxes.

One is called an **income tax.** It's a percentage of a person's salary that goes to the government.

Another type of tax is called a **sales tax.** It's a small percentage of money that is added to the price when we buy any goods or service. Like we pay sales tax when we buy a toy, a book or when we eat in restaurants.

Taxes are important because they help to strengthen our community.

They pay for things we all need, like parks to play in and firefighters to keep us safe.

CHAPTER 5

INTERNATIONAL TRADE

At lunch, you swapped the chips you got for lunch out for your friend's cookie.

You both exchanged what you had for what you wanted. This is the basic concept of trade.

Similarly, countries exchange goods and services between themselves. This is called **international trade.**

When a country sends goods out of the country, they **export.** This means they sell products they make to other countries.

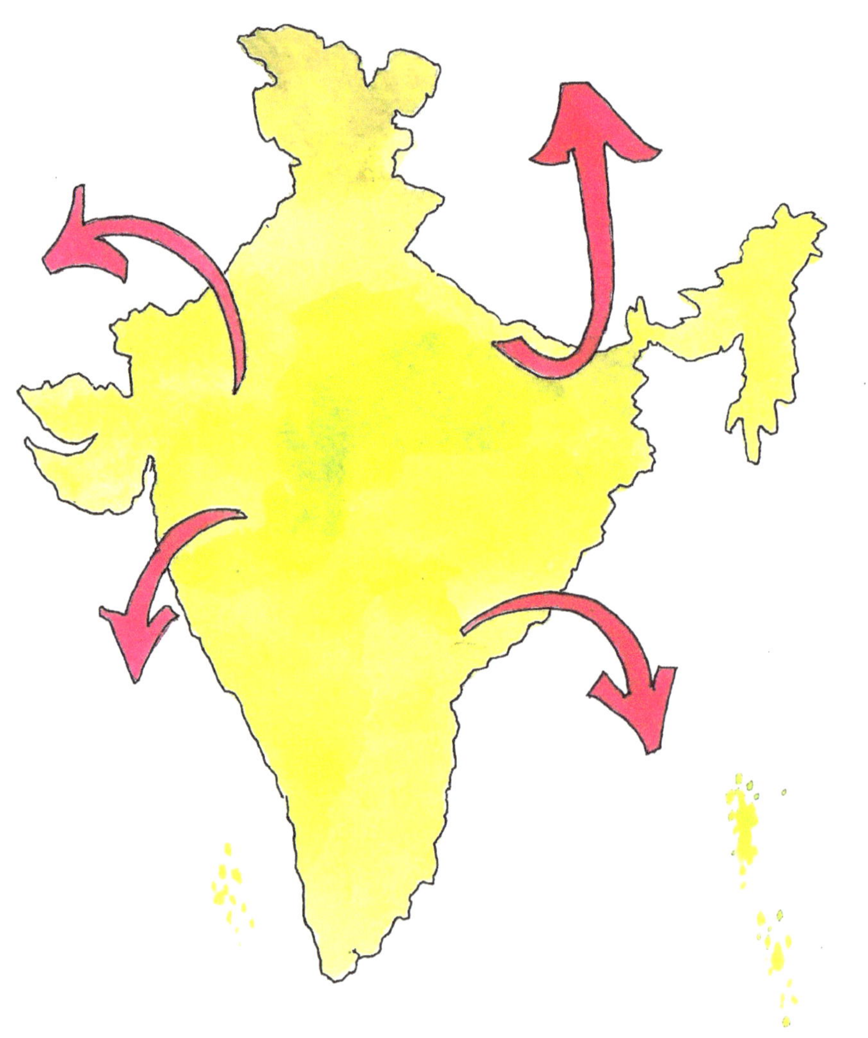

For example, India exports tea, spices, and textiles to countries around the world.

On the other hand, **importing** is when a country buys goods from other countries.

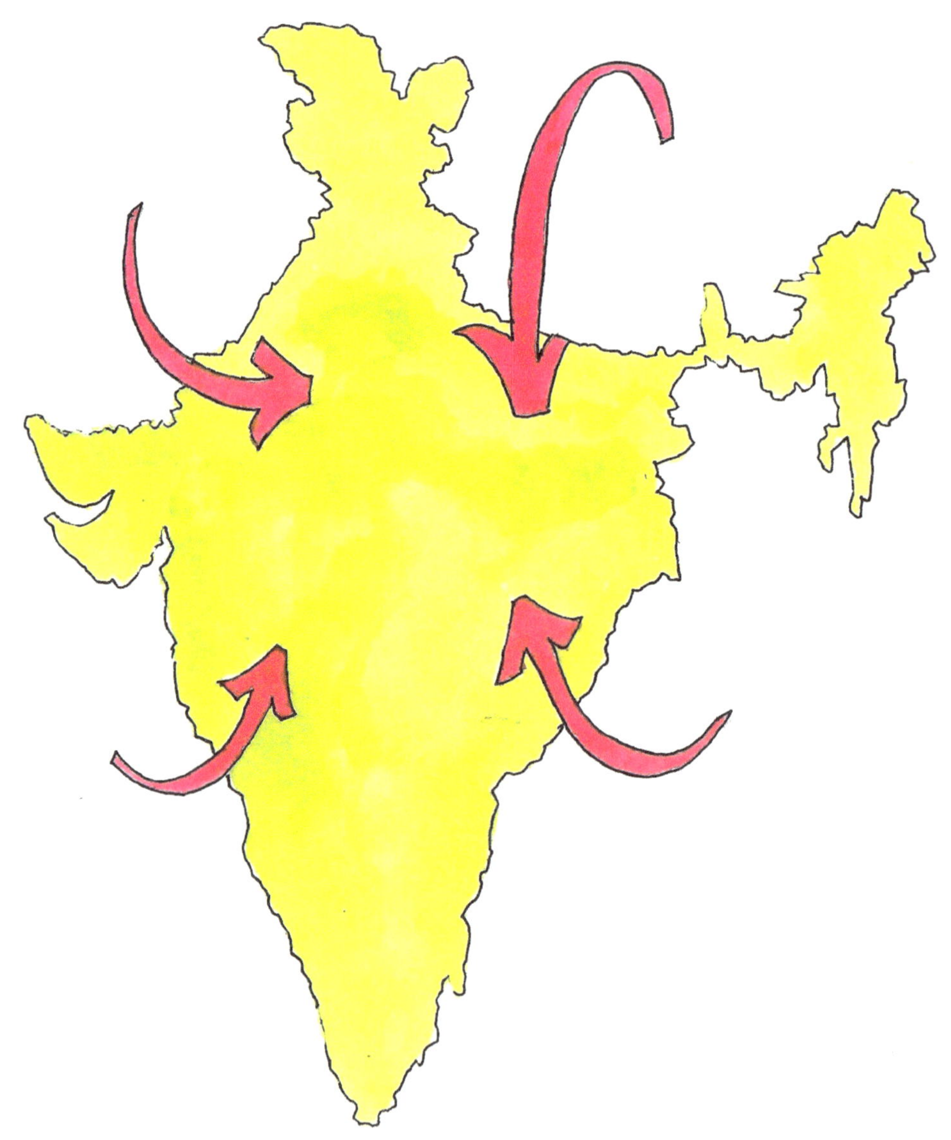

This could be things like electronics, machinery, or even fruits that don't grow locally.

International trade is crucial because it allows countries to access a wider variety of goods and services.

It also helps countries specialise in what they are best at producing and provides consumers with more choices and better prices.

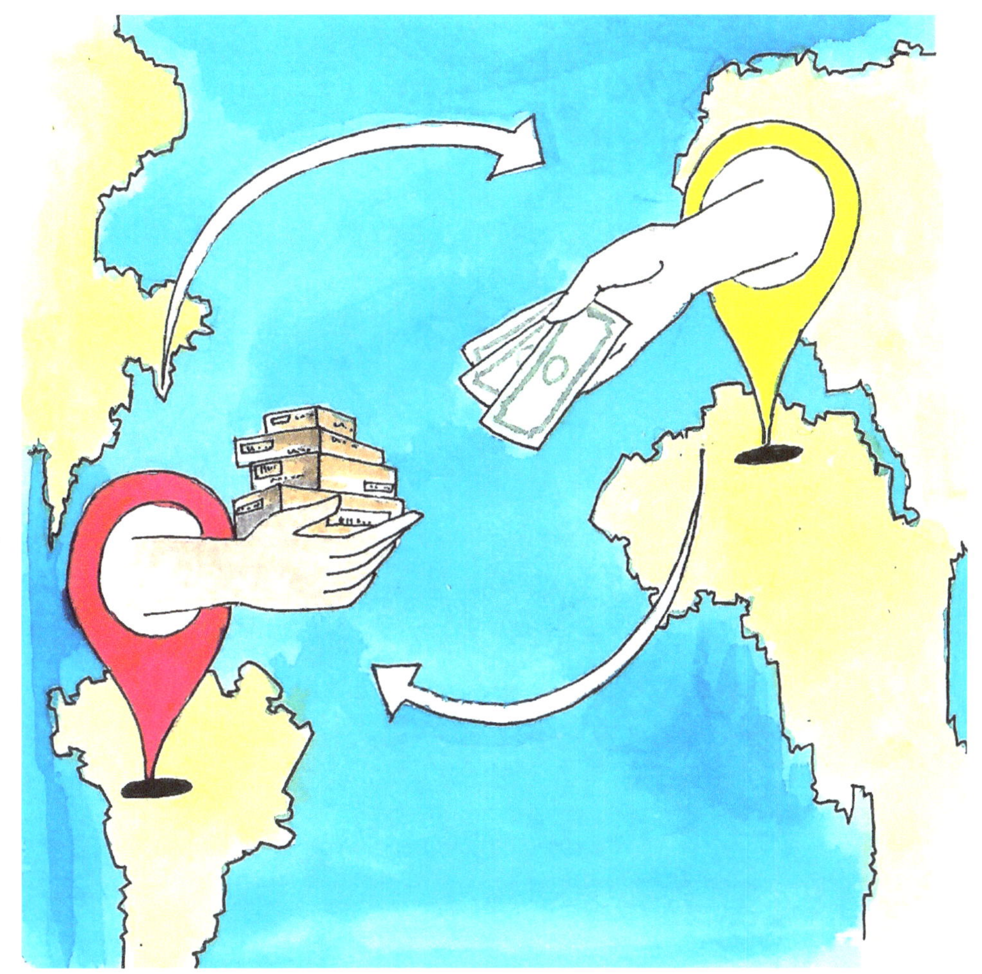

Just like how trading with your friends can be fun and beneficial, international trade helps countries grow and develop by sharing and exchanging what they have with others.

CHAPTER 6:

TEST YOUR KNOWLEDGE!

1. Imagine you are starting a lemonade stand! Here are some things you might need. Can you separate them into the right categories of factors of production? Put each item in the right category: Land, Labor, Capital, or Entrepreneurship.

   - A small table or stand
   - Your friend helping you squeeze lemons
   - A spot in your yard to set up the stand
   - A juicer
   - Access to water
   - Your idea to start a lemonade stand
   - A sibling handling money
   - Pitchers and cups
   - Business strategies to help get customers
   - A nearby park to set up the stand

2. Imagine a kid comes to your lemonade stand with 30 rupees. They tell you they can either buy a cup of lemonade from you for 30 rupees or buy a toy with that money later. What is the opportunity cost of choosing to buy the lemonade?

3. It's a really cold day, and not many people want a cup of lemonade. You're ready with 20 cups of lemonade to sell, but you only have 4 customers asking for a cup each.

    - The supply is _________ cups
    - The demand is _________ cups
    - This situation is called (surplus/shortage) _________.

4. You spend some time researching ways to increase the demand without changing the price. You come up with a list of strategies you can use as shown below. Can you name each strategy?

- Giving combo-deals such as buy 3 get 1 free
- Posting about your stand on social media so more people know about it
- Making unique, special flavours like pink lemonade, strawberry-watermelon lemonade, and spiced lemonade

5. Factors of production are needed for any business to run. Firms buy them from households and give something in return. Can you match each factor of production to what firms give in return for it?

Land	Interest
Labour	Rent
Capital	Profits
Entrepreneurship	Wages

6. We pay taxes from our income and on goods and services we buy as well. This money goes to the government. Why do we pay taxes?

7. Country A produces lots of bananas, but it does not produce very many toys. On the other hand, Country B is very good at producing toys but does not have the natural resources to grow bananas. Let's help Country A out!

- Country A should (import/export) _______ bananas to country B
- Country A should (import/export) _______ toys from country B